Tarantulas

Tarantulas

THE BIGGEST SPIDERS

Alexander L. Crosby

WALKER AND COMPANY  New York

Library of Congress Cataloging in Publication Data

Crosby, Alexander L.
  Tarantulas, the biggest spiders.

  Includes index.
  SUMMARY: Discusses the habits and characteristics
of the large and mildly poisonous tarantulas.
  1. Tarantulas—Juvenile literature. [1. Tarantulas.
2. Spiders] I. Title.
QL458.42.T5C76   1981   595.4′4   80–7672

ISBN 0-8027–6393–6
ISBN 0-8027–6394–4 (lib. bdg.)

PHOTO AND ILLUSTRATION CREDITS

American Museum of Natural History p. 8
Don Anderson—*Bellingham Herald* p. 55
Alice Gray pp. 56, 59
Ann Moreton p. 15
Lee Passmore—San Diego, California pp. 11, 12, 14, 18, 25, 26, 27, 28, 29,
    41, 60
Dr. Edward S. Ross—California Academy of Sciences pp. 21, 44, 47, 48, 49
San Diego Historical Society p. 39
Jean Zallinger pp. 16, 17

Text copyright © 1981 by Estate of Alexander L. Crosby

First published in the United States of America in 1981 by
the Walker Publishing Company, Inc.

Published simultaneously in Canada by Beaverbooks, Limited,
Don Mills, Ontario.

Trade ISBN: 0-8027-6393-6   Reinf. ISBN: 0-8027-6394-4

Library of Congress Catalog Card Number: 80-7672

Printed in the United States of America

10 9 8 7 6 5 4 3 2 1

Book designed by Lena Fong Hor

Thanks to Dale Lund
of the American Tarantula Society
for reading the text of this book.

Contents

The Biggest Spider.. 9

New Families 23

Not So Dangerous 33

The Lost Colony 37

The Deadliest Enemy...45

Tarantulas as Pets 51

Index..63

MEXICAN TARANTULA

The Biggest Spider

ONE NIGHT I was driving along a gravel road in a canyon near San Diego. Suddenly the headlights showed a small black creature crossing the road. I stopped quickly. A tarantula was taking its time to reach the sagebrush. I spread my handkerchief on the gravel and gently pushed the tarantula onto it, then carried it to a safe place.

The tarantula is the biggest spider in the United States. Although some kinds are big enough to kill small frogs and snakes, most feed on beetles, crickets, grasshoppers, and other small creatures.

There are about 100 species of tarantulas in North America. Their bodies are up to 2¾ inches (7 centimeters) long and the leg span runs to about 5 inches (12.7 centimeters).

Many people are afraid of tarantulas because they are large and mildly poisonous. (Their bite is no worse than a bee sting.) But the tarantula has made many friends in recent years. It generally has a good disposition and does not bite people. It does not destroy vegetable or flower gardens but eats some of the bugs that do. The female may live for twenty years or more and become a household pet. The male has a much shorter life-span.

Tarantulas are found from Missouri to California and in many foreign countries. They like a warm climate. Mexico has many kinds of tarantulas, some of them brightly ornamented with red or orange. In Central America they often live in banana trees. Each year a few reach the United States, hidden in large bunches of bananas.

In the United States and Mexico a tarantula lives in a hole it has dug, sometimes beneath a rock but usually in the open. The hole goes straight down for a few inches and then becomes level for a foot or two. The entrance is lined with silk that the tarantula spins. Silk gives a foothold as the spider moves around. At the end of the hole there is some extra room. This is where the female spider builds her egg sac.

TARANTULA NEST

CLOSE-UP OF TARANTULA NEST SHOWING
TARANTULA, CAST SKIN AND EGG CASES

Some tarantulas in California make a ring of grass and twigs around the burrow entrance. It is like a thick doughnut. The tarantula will then sit on top and wait for a careless insect to pass by.

Tarantulas live in colonies that are not altogether safe for them because these spiders sometimes eat each other. Yet the eyesight of a tarantula is so poor that it cannot see a juicy neighbor only two or three feet away.

Like all spiders, the tarantula has no inner skeleton to support its body. Everything is held together by a tough outer skin. The skin is shed as the spider grows, and a new skin takes its place. This is called *molting*. A young spider molts about four times a year. In three years it will be four times larger. A mature spider of ten or twelve years gets a new skin once a year.

Getting rid of the old skin is harder than pulling off a T-shirt that is one size too small. The process takes four or five hours. The tarantula picks a sheltered spot such as its own burrow. At first it lies on its back and wiggles the legs from time to time. Then it makes a half turn to its side and begins to pull and push its way out of the old skin. This is a slow and tedious job. When it is finished, there seem to be two tarantulas. One is the old skin, which is still in one piece.

TARANTULA MOLTING. IT IS LYING ON ITS BACK AND
WITHDRAWING ITS LEGS FROM THE OLD COVERINGS.

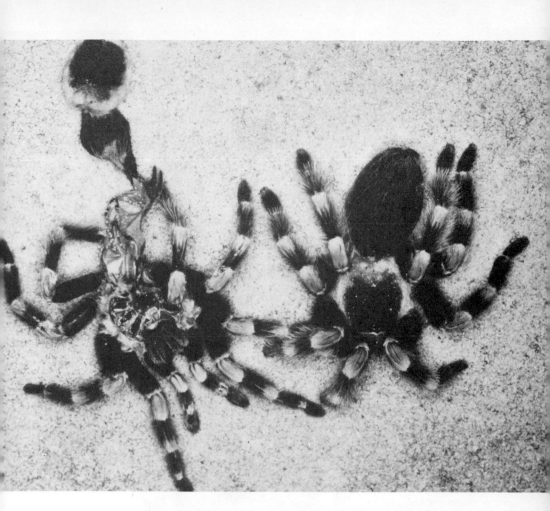

THE TARANTULA IS ON THE RIGHT.
THE SHED SKIN IS ON THE LEFT.

Tired from the hard work, the tarantula will rest, often on top of the old skin. Then, like a cat washing a newborn kitten, it will clean itself. This must be done carefully, for the new skin is quite tender. If it breaks, the tarantula will bleed to death.

The tarantula's body has two main parts. The

15

front part is the *cephalothorax*, which includes the head and the thorax. It is protected by a hard shell, the *carapace.*

The rear part is the *abdomen.* Most of the internal organs are here, including the silk glands.

The eight eyes of the tarantula are so small you would hardly notice them. They are at the front of the carapace, just above the mouth.

The *chelicerae* (sometimes called jaws) are used for eating and digging. The tarantula will grab a grasshopper with them and hold it for sucking. The

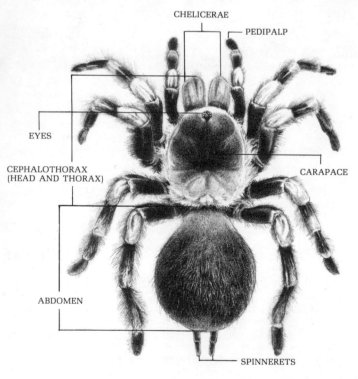

TOP VIEW OF TARANTULA

chelicerae are also used to move dirt in making a burrow. At the ends of the chelicerae are the spider's fangs, which get poison from glands inside the body.

Next to the chelicerae are the *pedipalps,* which look like two short legs. They are used to carry food to the tarantula's mouth and as feelers in walking. The spider depends more on touch than on sight.

Like all spiders, the tarantula has four pairs of legs. They are covered with hair, and they have small claws at the ends. You can feel the claws when a tarantula walks on your arm. The claws won't hurt

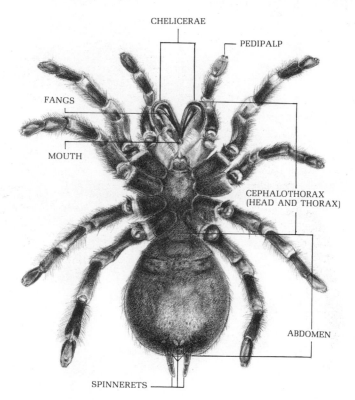

BOTTOM VIEW OF TARANTULA

CLOSE-UP OF CHELICERAE

you, but they keep the tarantula from slipping. A fall to the floor can kill a tarantula, which is one reason why a pet spider should not be handled much.

Two small organs at the rear of the tarantula are the *spinnerets*. Microscopic tubes from the silk glands bring silk to these organs, which the tarantula aims where it wishes.

Silk is very important to tarantulas. In the mating season the male spins a sheet of silk, covering a small hollow in the ground or stretching between two small stones. On this sheet he deposits a drop of seminal fluid. The drop is then picked up by his pedipalps in a rapid dipping that lasts more than an hour. The fluid is used in mating with a female.

Nobody knows how a male tarantula finds a female in the fall mating season. Tarantulas are so nearly blind that they cannot see anything just a few inches away. Possibly the male has a keen sense of smell and can tell whether a female is nearby. So he goes to the burrow where the female is waiting.

If the female is friendly, she welcomes her guest. She stands on her four hind legs for an embrace. The male also rises on his hind legs and inserts the tips of his pedipalps into her sexual opening. In two or three minutes the mating is usually finished. The male then leaves promptly, for the female may attack him.

No eggs will be laid until early the following summer. Then the female makes a silken sheet and lays up to one thousand eggs on it. She folds the edges together to make a cocoon, which she guards carefully until the tiny spiders come out.

Even though tarantulas do not spin outdoor webs to catch insects, the webs in front of a burrow will bring some meals. The spider will investigate any vibration in the silk. Often it comes from a struggling beetle or grasshopper.

In the burrow, silk is used like wallpaper. The silk comes wet from the spinnerets but dries immediately.

Tarantulas eat no solid food. They live on a liquid diet. Instead of trying to break up and chew the shell of a beetle, they make a hole and suck the juice.

A large tarantula can eat a mouse, but not so fast as a cat. The meal will take up to two days. The tarantula's digestive juices go into the mouse and liquefy the soft parts. If it is a baby mouse, with no firm bones, only a tiny pellet will be left.

Like other spiders, the tarantula is a slow eater. When a grasshopper is captured in the tarantula's fangs, the spider puts its very small mouth against the victim's body and sucks for about fifteen minutes. Then it will move to another position. The meal may continue for five hours or even longer. About every

TARANTULA FEEDING ON A CRICKET

half hour the tarantula stops to rest. It will drop the
insect and take a very short walk. When the meal is
finished, the grasshopper will be a small lump made
from the parts that cannot be liquefied.

Nobody yet knows whether a tarantula can hear

or smell. One thing is clear: The tarantula wants things that are alive. It will eat most kinds of insects and spiders, but it may walk away from a cockroach that just doesn't taste good. In New York City, however, a man solved the problem of cockroaches in his apartment. He turned his tarantula loose, and the roaches vanished.

The tarantula got its name from the city of Taranto, on the southern coast of Italy. In the fifteenth century, the people there blamed a large spider for a strange disease called tarantism, after the town. The person bitten was said to die unless he went into a wild dance with special music. This kind of medical treatment led to the Italian folk dance the tarantella, which is still popular.

The Italian tarantula was not the tarantula found in the United States and Latin America. It was a European wolf spider, which was big but not poisonous. Maybe the people of Taranto were wild about music and dancing and sometimes needed an excuse to stop work and have a good time.

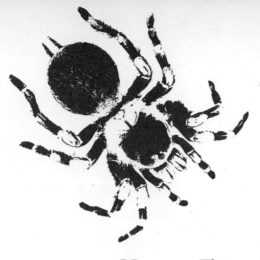

New Families

TARANTULAS TAKE ALMOST as much time to start a new family as people take. The female is not ready to be a mother until she is ten to twelve years old.

The foremost authority on tarantulas, Dr. William J. Baerg, raised many hundreds and observed hundreds more in the field. In his book *The Tarantula* he tells how the male tarantulas seek females in Kansas:

Beginning with the first of October it was easy to find males cruising about on the hillside, where they were presumably looking for females. Some males I saw were sitting patiently in front of females' holes. One of them was vigorously tapping on the silken cover of a hole, his way of ringing the doorbell. I did not observe mating in the field; presumably it takes place in the hole or under a stone.

The males are apt to mate several times during the season. After mating they get weaker. They lose interest in food or water. They do not move much. They fold their legs beneath them and soon die from old age.

The female's life is different from that of the male. After four or five males have mated with her, she goes into her burrow and plugs the entrance with dirt. She does not gather food, for she waits until spring before eating. The main thing is to keep out the winter cold.

By March or April she has moved the dirt from her front door and is sitting in the sunshine. She will eat the first insects that pass by.

Late in June she will build the cocoon that will hold her eggs. This work is done in the burrow, out of sight.

Dr. Baerg wanted to see how a tarantula's cocoon was put together, so he brought into his laboratory five females who were heavy with eggs.

The best spinner began just before 8 A.M. by laying down a small sheet of silk in her jar. She spun for three hours without resting. Then she rested a few seconds every three to five minutes. After seven hours of spinning, she had a neat cradle 2½ inches (6.35

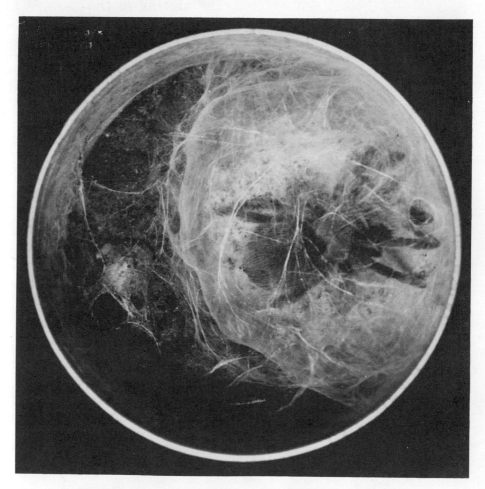

THE TARANTULA SPINS A SILKY WEB THAT
PROTECTS ITS EGGS FROM MOLD.

centimeters) wide and 5 inches (12.7 centimeters)
long.

She kept on spinning for more than two hours.
Her cocoon had to be thick enough for its cargo of
eggs. Finally she settled down on the cradle and began

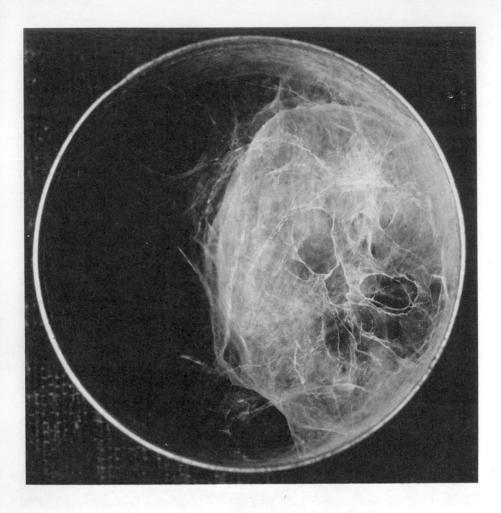

THE CEILING OF WEB HERE IS TOO THICK TO
SHOW THE TARANTULA.

laying eggs. It took only fifteen minutes to deposit the
average 650 yellowish green eggs. That was one egg
every second and a half.

Then she began to spin a covering for the eggs. After
two hours she was pulling the silken sheet down over

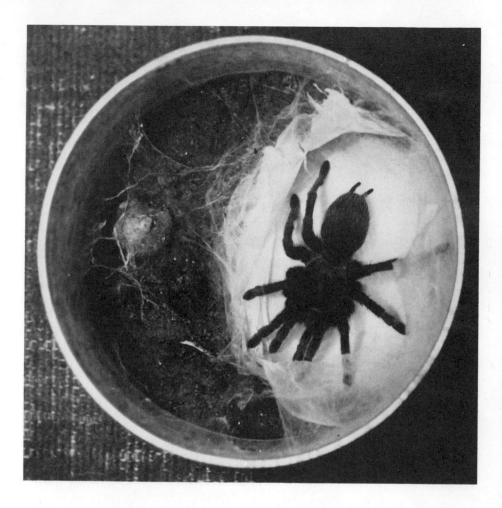

THE TARANTULA IS PULLING THE SILKY
THREADS DOWN AROUND THE EGGS.

the eggs. The final job was to seal the edges of the
cocoon.

But the tarantula did not seem satisfied with her
work. Instead of being the usual globe about one inch
in diameter, the cocoon was a long sack. The spider

THE EGGS ARE ROLLED INTO A SILKY BALL.

tried to make the cocoon rounder by turning it over and patting it with her legs. She gave up at 11 P.M., after fifteen hours of work.

Dr. Baerg was ready for bed. He has suggested that anyone who wishes to see a cocoon being built should bring both lunch and supper with him.

Cocoons made in the tarantula's own burrow are smoother and rounder than those built in a jar in the laboratory. And they probably take less time—even though there is less space for the spinner.

Each cocoon holds up to one thousand eggs and is carefully guarded by the female. Sometimes she will bring it to the sunshine at the entrance of her burrow. If a visitor comes close enough to be seen, she will quickly carry it back.

TARANTULA AND EGGS
IN THE NEST

Dr. Baerg used a weed stalk to find out whether a tarantula had a cocoon in her burrow. If there was one, the spider would grab the weed. If none she would ignore it.

Although the female is a fighter, she gives up when ants invade her burrow. The insects will tear open a cocoon to get the eggs and any baby spiders that have hatched. There will be too many ants for the tarantula to fight. She will back away and then abandon her home.

When no ants or other raiders come, the young tarantulas leave the eggshells in about three weeks, but they stay in the cocoon for several weeks longer. The newborn are white, unlike their dark gray or brown parents. By late August, when they are ready to leave the cocoon, the spiderlings have turned light brown.

How do more than five hundred tiny spiders get out of a silken cocoon? Two or three small holes are bitten through the silk. The spiderlings then spend a day or two crawling out, one by one.

The newborn young of many web-spinning spiders are carried great distances on silk threads blown by the wind. This does not happen with tarantulas. The babies venture only yards from the burrow where they were born. And they travel on their own legs, not by air.

The spiderlings are only one sixth of an inch (.042 millimeters) long, which is too small to keep track of. When they grow larger, they may be seized by birds and wasps. A wasp does not eat her catch. Instead, she feeds it to the larvae that hatch from her eggs.

For about six months after hatching, the young spiders need no food, but their appetites get strong in the springtime. In Dr. Baerg's laboratory, they began to eat the nearest snack: another spiderling. This cannibalism lasted for almost three months. By that time one family of more than five hundred had only fifteen tough fighters left.

Dr. Baerg did not want all of the spiderlings eaten, so he put the survivors in four smaller jars. Then he gathered insects for their meals. Termites were the main diet. These wood eaters had nests in the ground at the foot of a tree. They had built tubes up the bark to some dead wood. Dr. Baerg would break open a tube and brush a dozen or so termites into a jar. These were fed to the spiderlings once or twice a week. Water was given on absorbent cotton in a small dish.

The baby tarantulas needed no food during the cold months, November through March. They got a drink of water every other week.

In their first three years they grew from one sixth

of an inch (.042 millimeters) to two thirds of an inch (.252 millimeters) in length, making them long enough to cover a dime.

After four years the young tarantulas were big enough to eat small grasshoppers, crickets, beetles, and an occasional caterpillar. Two or three years later they were feeding on large grasshoppers, cicadas, and June beetles.

A hungry tarantula will eat a tent caterpillar. Some landowners would be happy if they had thousands of tarantulas eating the caterpillars that strip the leaves from their trees.

Not So Dangerous

THE GREAT FRENCH entomologist Jean Henri Fabre, who was born in 1823 and lived until 1915, was particularly interested in tarantulas. How did they kill the insects and small animals that they ate? How poisonous were they?

Fabre went to the tarantulas to get the answers. He did not have to go far. Only a block from his house in Sérigan, Provence, was some wasteland, once a vineyard, with at least one hundred burrows. He took some small bottles with necks that were wide enough to cover the entrance to a tarantula's hole. In each bottle he put a carpenter bee, which is larger than a bumblebee and has a very painful sting. Then he watched to see what would happen.

Four times a tarantula was aroused by the buzzing of the bee in a bottle. But each time the spider backed down when she saw the huge bee. Perhaps she sensed that the bee was dangerous and the bottle would not be an easy place to fight. At the fifth hole the story told by Fabre was different:

A Spider suddenly rushes from her hole: she has been rendered warlike, doubtless, by prolonged abstinence. The tragedy that happens under the cover of the bottle lasts for but the twinkling of an eye. It is over: the sturdy carpenter bee is dead. Where did the murderess strike her? That is easily ascertained: the tarantula has not let go; and her fangs are planted in the nape of the neck. The assassin has the knowledge which I suspected: she has made for the essentially vital center, she has stung the insect's cervical ganglia with her poison fangs.

Two other tarantulas killed bees in exactly the same place.

Fabre's next experiment was with a young sparrow, ready to fly. He had a tarantula bite the bird's leg. The leg was quickly crippled; the sparrow had to hop upon the other leg. But its appetite was good, and Fabre's daughters fed it on flies, bread crumbs, and apricot pulp. Everybody in the family expected the sparrow to recover. But after two days it refused food, had spasms, and died.

Fabre wrote that there was "a certain coolness among us at the evening meal." His family was saddened by the sparrow's death and felt that Fabre had been cruel. The entomologist admitted that he did not feel good himself. "I am not made of the stuff of those who, without turning a hair, rip up live dogs to find out nothing in particular," he said.

One more experiment was tried. Fabre had caught a mole that was pushing its way beneath a bed of lettuce. He put the mole into a large cage and fed it beetles and grasshoppers, which were quickly eaten. Then he put a tarantula in the cage. The mole was bitten on its snout. It began to scratch its nose. It lost interest in eating and in thirty-six hours died.

Fabre concluded after these experiments that the bite of a French tarantula is "not an accident which man can afford to treat lightly."

But there is nothing to worry about if you are bitten by a North American tarantula. Charles F. Harbison of the Natural History Museum in San Diego was bitten at eleven different times. Only once did he have a slight swelling. All the other times there was no more pain than if he had had two pin pricks.

A biting tarantula may have a bad disposition, like the kind of dog that bites when it is petted. However, Baerg had one tarantula that was so friendly it had to be coaxed into biting for an experiment. Harbison's tarantulas were generally slow to bite.

Fairy tales about spiders have been told for thousands of years. Alexander the Great heard about a beautiful woman in Egypt who had eaten spiders since she was a little girl. The king was warned not to embrace her, lest he be poisoned by venom that might evaporate from her sweat.

In Mexico many people believe that tarantulas bite horses just above the hoof. The hoof then drops off, the horse dies, and the tarantula uses horsehair to line its nest. An interesting story, but it has never happened.

Panamanians call tarantulas "antelopes" because they are supposed to be great jumpers. Few tarantulas ever jump at all, just as they don't bite horses. But they often live in houses in tropical countries. They don't bother the people, who are pleased to have the tarantulas eat the house bugs.

The Lost Colony

EVEN IN TARANTULA country, finding a tarantula is a matter of luck. You can walk for miles and not see one. You may never find a colony where a dozen or more females have dug their burrows.

Probably no scientist has searched for tarantulas as thoroughly as Dr. William J. Baerg did. He traveled through the Southwest, and he explored many parts of Latin America.

In 1926 Dr. Baerg went to Mexico. In the state of Durango he was driving along a country road near the Bermejillo railroad station. Suddenly he jammed on his brakes. A huge tarantula was crossing the road and going into the sagebrush.

Baerg jumped out of his car. What he found was "the biggest colony of the biggest tarantulas I had ever seen in all my years of searching."

The colony was near the headquarters of the Tlahualilo Ranch, which covered some sixty thousand acres. On this ancient lake bed, the irrigated crops were cotton, wheat, and sorghum.

The tarantulas had settled in an uncultivated area of some twenty acres where the native mesquite grew. Many of the holes were only two or three feet apart.

The size of the tarantulas' bodies was up to about 85 millimeters, or 3¼ inches, not including legs. The weight was up to fifty-four grams, or almost two ounces.

The appetite of these big tarantulas was not dainty. Their menu included not only grasshoppers and beetles but also frogs, snakes, lizards, and crayfish. Baerg brought several Mexican tarantulas back to Kansas and fed them more than his other spiders required.

"Considering its size, this tarantula appears to be ponderous and slow-moving, but when it is hungry, I have seen it grab two large cicadas, one on each fang, in a small fraction of a second," Baerg wrote.

The Mexican tarantula was a medium brown with a greenish tint on the carapace. The scientist was

TARANTULA COUNTRY

especially pleased with the female, a long-lived creature that made a dependable pet.

Eight years later Baerg went back to Bermejillo to check on his great discovery. The visit was a sad one, for only a few tarantulas could be found. In 1954, after a twenty-year absence, Baerg returned again. He tramped over the dry ground for an hour or more, but he found only two tarantulas where thousands had once lived.

What had happened? There was no clear answer, but Baerg said that dry weather was probably one cause. Rainfall had dropped from about nine inches a year to three. Plants had shrunk or died. Because there was less food for plant-eating insects, most of them died. That meant less food for the tarantulas, and they also starved to death.

San Diego was "a paradise for tarantula hunters" in 1935, when Baerg and his wife drove there and were taken to the best tarantula areas by Lee Passmore, the photographer, who was a field naturalist.* A tarantula hunter has a tough time when he is in strange country with no guidance. He may spend weeks or even months without finding a single tarantula. After traveling with Passmore and seeing many tarantulas,

*A number of Passmore's photographs are in this book, through the courtesy of the Natural History Museum of San Diego.

WAITING FOR A NIGHT PICTURE IN
TARANTULA TERRITORY.

Baerg wrote: "My favorite region for studying those attractive creatures will always be San Diego."

Many of the colonies that Baerg visited in 1935 are now covered with asphalt, concrete, houses, lawns, chain stores, and beauty parlors. There is no mystery, as there was in Bermejillo, about what happened to the tarantulas. They were wiped out by bulldozers.

THE TARANTULA FACES THE ENEMY WASP.

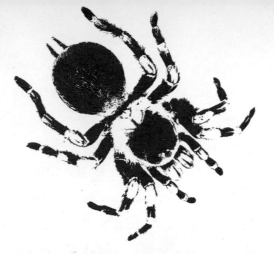

The Deadliest Enemy

AUTOMOBILES KILL many tarantulas when males search for females. Others are killed by nervous citizens who think tarantulas are as poisonous as black widow spiders. Still more are killed and eaten by other tarantulas, especially when they are young.

But the special enemy of the tarantula is the *Pepsis* wasp, a beautiful insect with russet wings and a deep blue body. It is known as the tarantula hawk.

When the wasp is ready to lay her single egg, she flies in search of the right tarantula. She may find a male hunting for a beetle. Or she may go into the dark burrow of a female.

If the wasp senses she has found the right breed

of tarantula, she attacks. The fight is usually short. The tarantula tries to back away, even though it is eight times heavier than its enemy.

Very rarely is the wasp injured. She knows where to sting. If the first sting does not paralyze the tarantula, she stings again, and the battle is over.

The tarantula is paralyzed, not killed. The wasp will drag it to a hole she has dug. There she will lay her egg beneath the spider's abdomen and glue it to the skin. Finally she covers the tarantula with dirt.

When the egg hatches, the larva feeds on the paralyzed spider. It changes into a pupa and finally becomes a wasp. Then it digs out of the hole.

When I was a boy in National City, California, my father once called me to a hillside sparsely covered with dry grass. He pointed to the ground. A paralyzed tarantula was being dragged by a tarantula hawk.

Two or three times the wasp left her burden and flew away for a minute or two. She was checking her route. When she returned, the tarantula drew in its legs slightly. The hawk grabbed hold and began backing again. She finally came to an old squirrel hole, where she dragged in the tarantula and laid her egg.

Few tarantulas ever survive an attack by *Pepsis.* But in Cuero, Texas, a woman who admires tarantulas

THE WASP GETS CLOSE.

saved one of them. Her dog had found the wasp dragging
a tarantula across the backyard. Mrs. Terry Gayle
Baecker got a jar, and the wasp backed into it, pulling
the tarantula. When Mr. Baecker came home, he took the

THE WASP INSERTS HER STINGER INTO THE TARANTULA
JUST BEHIND THE SECOND LEG.

THE WASP DRAGS THE PARALYZED TARANTULA
INTO THE TARANTULA'S HOLE.

tarantula away from the wasp and put it into a large jar
with sand.

For three months the tarantula remained paralyzed, but he finally began to recover. After a year he
was quite well, living in à big terrarium and enjoying
his food.

One country that no longer has tarantulas is Jamaica. Somebody got the bright idea of introducing the mongoose in 1872 to destory the rats that were destroying the sugar cane. The mongooses killed not only the rats but many other animals, including iguanas and tarantulas.

Tarantulas as Pets

TARANTULAS HAVE been kept as pets for longer than almost anyone would think. Leon Dufour, a French army surgeon, got interested in tarantulas when he was in Valencia, Spain, in 1812. He wrote,

> I caught a fair-sized male Tarantula, without hurting him, and imprisoned him in a glass jar, with a paper cover in which I cut a trap-door. At the bottom of the jar I put a paper bag, to serve as his habitual residence. I placed the jar on a table in my bedroom, so as to have him under frequent observation. He soon grew accustomed to captivity and ended by

51

*becoming so familiar that he would come
and take from my fingers the live fly
which I gave him. After killing his victim
with the fangs of his mandibles, he was
not satisfied, like most spiders, to suck
her head: he chewed her whole body,
shoving it piecemeal into his mouth with
his palpi, after which he threw up the
masticated teguments (the skin and other
hard parts) and swept them away from
his lodging.*

Dr. Baerg also liked tarantulas.

"After living with these creatures for several
years one becomes as fond of them as if they were
pets," Dr. Baerg wrote. "In fact, to me they are pets.
And I am not alone. There is the very young lad whom
I met briefly at Tlahualilo, Mexico, many years ago.
On his solemn request I gave him a partly grown
specimen. Twenty years later when I saw him again at
the Mexico City airport, he quickly reminded me of
the gift, saying that he had kept it for a long time.
'And,' his young wife added, 'he even took it along on
our honeymoon trip to London.'"

The gentlest tarantula that Dr. Baerg ever had
was named Curly. It was hard to get this lady to bite

anything for a test.

My high school friend, Charles F. Harbison, became a curator of entomology at the San Diego Natural History Museum. Once he visited us in Quakertown, Pennsylvania. My wife had invited several friends to come in that afternoon. Harbie—as he is known—said he had brought a friend, too. He got his bag, pulled out a large matchbox, and opened it. Inside was a tarantula.

Harbie gently lifted out the tarantula with his bare fingers and put her on his bare arm.

"This is Susie," he said.

Susie was so pleased to be out of the box that she began climbing Harbie's arm. When she got to the elbow, Harbie moved her back to the wrist. The spider started climbing again.

Everybody in the room was fascinated. Two persons who had never held a tarantula gave Susie a chance to crawl on their arms. Her touch was as gentle as that of a kitten. As a reward for good conduct, Harbie put several small beetles in her box that night. By morning, the beetles had been sucked dry.

The founder of the American Tarantula Society, Dale Lund, was extremely nervous about bugs in his childhood. When he was a teen-ager, he made up his mind to cure his fears—so he bought a tarantula.

Not knowing what to do with the fearsome spider, he wrote to the American Museum of Natural History in New York. Alice Gray, scientific assistant, sent him plenty of advice. Then, after years of experience, Lund wrote *All About Tarantulas,** which was published with handsome photographs in 1977. Early in 1978 he started the American Tarantula Society and its bimonthly newsletter, *Tarantula Times.* Membership has grown steadily to more than five hundred persons in less than two years.

Lund used to dread speech making even more than he did spiders. But he agreed to talk about tarantulas to the Alliance of Alien Prisoners at the federal penitentiary in Abbotsford, British Columbia. A salmon barbecue was the big outdoor meal. The prisoners gave such a warm reception to Lund, his wife, and their seven-month-old son that Lund tended to "feel safer with the prisoners than with the guards."

Tarantulas turn up in strange places. The West Side Association of Commerce in New York gave an award for community service to the American Museum of Natural History. Miss Gray accepted for the museum at a fancy dinner party. She said she could not have earned the award without the help of

*The book may be ordered for $2.95, postpaid, from the American Tarantula Society, Box 2312, Bellingham, Washington 98225.

54

DALE LUND WITH HIS PET TARANTULA "ALICE BROWN"

ALICE GRAY WITH HER PET TARANTULA "BLONDIE"

her arthropod team, and she would like to introduce the senior member. She opened a small brass box, neatly polished, and lifted out her favorite tarantula, Blondie. "After an incredulous pause, we got a standing ovation," Miss Gray reported.

It is hard to guess how many people own tarantulas. One experienced owner thinks there is a pet tarantula in one house out of every thousand. That could be true in communities where tarantulas are sold in pet shops.

Why couldn't more tarantulas be bred, like dogs and chickens? The only person known for raising tarantulas from eggs to maturity is Dr. William J. Baerg. Most household pets mature in about a year— but not a tarantula. It spends from a few years to up to twelve years growing up. Hardly anyone will spend ten or twelve years feeding a growing spider.

Many kinds of captured tarantulas are sold in pet shops throughout the United States. Prices in 1980 ran from about eight dollars to forty dollars.

Feeding a pet tarantula is a problem when live food is scarce. Pet stores have crickets from time to time—but never enough. No beetles, no grasshoppers. Dr. Bill Jackson, a psychiatrist in Madison, Wisconsin, found a solution for his tarantula, Spot. He took a one-inch-long fish from his aquarium and dropped it into the spider's terrarium. Spot jumped on it immediately and sucked it nearly dry.

The tarantula had no trouble later in eating fish several inches long. He would stand on the wriggling fish and give it a dose of his mild poison.

Dr. Jackson next taught Spot how to catch fish from water. At first the fish would be put in the empty water dish. After the tarantula had helped himself several times, 1/10-inch of water was added. The spider, known for his dislike of water, did not object. Next he went after fishes in water 1/4-inch deep, and finally he hooked fishes swimming in a depth of 1/2 inch.

When there are no crickets and no fishes, a tarantula may be fooled into accepting hamburger. A small pellet of the ground meat is wrapped around the end of a thread. The morsel is jiggled before the tarantula, which will grab almost anything that looks alive. The thread should then be gently pulled until the tarantula pulls harder and gets her meal.

Tarantulas do not overeat, and they are able to go several months without eating at all. However, anyone who has a pet tarantula should give it a cricket or two every few days. During the winter season no food is needed, but an occasional drink of water will be welcome.

"BLONDIE" HARNESSED FOR APPEARANCE ON TV

The world's only spider museum is on County Road 614, outside of Powhatan, Virginia. Ann Moreton, a photographer and writer, operates the museum in the historic Woodward Mill from April 1 through October 31. Her rarest exhibit is *Listiphus desultar,* a Mongolian tarantula that had not been seen for 125 years. A contemporary specimen was found in 1972 by Dr. W. S. Bristowe of England, who had gone to Penang, Mongolia, to hunt for it. These spiders have orange and black legs and very little poison.

Although tarantulas cannot see more than a very few inches, at least one tarantula could tell colors apart. Theodore Brunette of Coraopolis, Pennsylvania, reported that he put mixed gravel of red, white, and green into the tank used by his Mexican Red Leg. After about four hours the spider separated the gravel into piles for each color. Later Brunette added a tiny automobile about one inch long. The tarantula studied this object and then buried it.

Tarantulas have a new role in the business world: They are being used as guardians of jewelry stores. One tarantula is left in each display case at night, and warning signs are posted. Since most people fear them, burglars are apt to leave the jewelry alone.

The new system was first used by a San Francisco store. It is now promoted on the East Coast by Tarantula Enterprises of New Milford, New Jersey, which rents the spiders. The president of the firm is John G. Browning, author of a new book about tarantulas published by T. F. H. Publications.

Another friend of tarantulas is Rick West, a Canadian. He took his bride, Lynn, on a honeymoon in the San Diego desert country. While he was hunting along the road with a flashlight, there was a terrifying scream from his car. West ran back. One of his tarantulas had escaped from a box and climbed up his wife's leg. The gentle spider had not taken a nibble.

Despite tarantula hawk wasps, automobiles, and tarantulas that eat their own relatives, these big spiders are going to be with us for centuries. They have found a new friend: *homo sapiens,* which includes you.

INDEX

Abdomen, 16
Age, 23
American Tarantula
    Society, 53, 54, 62
Ants, 30

Baerg, Dr. William J., 23,
    24, 26, 28, 29, 31, 36, 37,
    38, 40, 52, 57
Bee, 34
Bite, 10, 35-36
Body structure, 13, 15-19
Burrow, 13, 20, 24, 30, 33

Carapace, 16
Carpenter bee, 33-34
Cephalothorax, 16
Chelicerae (jaws), 16-17
Claws, 17

Cocoon, 10, 20, 24, 25, 27-
    30
Colonies, 13, 37-38, 40
Color, 10
    recognition of, 61

Eating habits, 20, 21
Egg sac. See Cocoon
Eggs, 20, 24, 26-29
Enemies, 45
Eyes, 16
Eyesight, 13, 16, 61

Fabre, Jean Henri, 33-35
Families, 23
Female, 19, 23, 24
Fighting techniques, 33,
    34, 38
Food, 9, 10, 20, 22, 57, 58

Gray, Alice, 54, 56-57
Guardians of jewelry, 61

Habitat, 10, 11, 12, 13
Harbison, Charles F.,
    35-36, 53

Jaws. *See* Chelicerae

Legs, 17, 19
Life span, 10
Lund, Dale, 53, 54

Male, 19, 23, 24, 45
Mating, 19, 23-24
Mexican tarantulas, 38
    40, 61
Mexico, 10, 36, 37, 52
Molting, 13-15
Mongoose, 50
Nest. *See* Habitat

Passmore, Lee, 40
Pedipalps. *See* Legs
Pepsis wasp, 45-49
Pet tarantulas, 10, 51-62

San Diego, 9, 40, 53
Silk, 10, 19, 20, 24
Size, 9-10
Skin. *See* Molting
Sparrow, 34-35
Spider museum, 58, 61
Spiderlings, 30-32
Spinnerets, 19

Taranto, Italy, 22
Tarantula hawk. *See*
    Pepsis wasp

Wasps, 31. *See also* Pepsi
    wasp
Wolf spider, 22